MY BEST BOOK OF
SPACESHIPS

Ian Graham

KINGFISHER
KNOW | WONDER
www.kingfisherbooks.com

KINGFISHER
LONDON & NEW YORK

Copyright © Macmillan Publishers International Ltd 2005, 2018
First published 1995 in the United States by Kingfisher
This edition published 2018 by Kingfisher
175 Fifth Ave., New York, NY 10010
Kingfisher is an imprint of Macmillan Children's Books, London
All rights reserved.

Distributed in the U.S. and Canada by Macmillan,
175 Fifth Ave., New York, NY 10010

Library of Congress Cataloging-in-Publication data has been
applied for.

ISBN 978-0-7534-7463-1

Design by Wildpixel Ltd.
Illustrations: Ray Grinaway, Roger Stewart

Kingfisher books are available for special promotions and
premiums. For details contact: Special Markets Department,
Macmillan, 175 Fifth Ave., New York, NY 10010

For more information please visit
www.kingfisherbooks.com

Printed in China
9 8 7 6 5 4 3 2 1
1TR/0618/UNTD/WKT/128MA

Picture credits
The Publisher would like to thank the following for permission
to reproduce their material.
Top = t; Bottom = b; Center = c; Left = l; Right = r
Cover, page 1, 8–9, 16–17, 18 iStock/3DSculptor; 2–3, 32 iStock/
blinow61; 4–5 iStock/Nick Pandevonium; 4b Shutterstock/Triff;
14 background Shutterstock/Castleski; 19b Shutterstock/robert_s;
20 Shutterstock/Johan Swanepoel; 26–27 background Shutterstock/
JaySi; 28–29 Shutterstock/Guitar photographer; 30–31 background
Shutterstock/Dima Zel; all other photographs NASA.

CONTENTS

Looking into space 4

What's in space? 6

Blast off! 8

All types of rockets 10

Going to the Moon 12

Apollo spacecraft 14

Space stations 16

The space shuttle 18

Shuttle power 20

Working in space 22

Space suits 24

Eyes in space 26

The Hubble Telescope 28

Space probes 30

Glossary and index 32

LOOKING INTO SPACE

For thousands of years, people have gazed in wonder at the night sky. Slowly, they learned more and more about the twinkling stars and the planets above them. Many dreamed of visiting and exploring the planets, but there was no way of traveling there. Instead, people had to make do with fuzzy views seen through telescopes. Nowadays, we have all types of spacecraft that can travel into space, visit the planets, and even land on them.

Robot explorers

Robot explorers, like the Mars rover, have become our eyes and ears on distant worlds we have not yet visited ourselves.

WHAT'S IN SPACE?

Earth is one of eight planets that fly through space around the Sun. The path that each planet follows as it flies around the Sun is called an orbit. Earth takes one year to orbit the Sun once. The Sun is enormous. One million Earths could fit inside it with lots of room to spare.

The Sun is the star at the center of our solar system.

Mercury is the closest planet to the Sun.

Venus is a scorching-hot planet where it rains acid.

Earth is our home planet.

Mars is a red and rocky planet that humans may visit in the near future.

Jupiter is the biggest planet in the solar system.

The pull of gravity

Gravity is an invisible force that pulls things toward it. The Sun is so big, its pull of gravity is strong enough to hold all the planets in their orbits.

The solar system

The solar system is the name given to the Sun's family. It includes the planets and their moons, comets, and all the lumps of rock, dust, and ice that orbit the Sun.

Far, far beyond our galaxy are other galaxies containing billions of stars.

Asteroids are large chunks of space rock and metal. The asteroid belt is an area between Jupiter and Saturn where millions of asteroids are in orbit.

Saturn is a planet surrounded by beautiful rings.

Uranus is a planet tipped over on its side.

Neptune is a beautiful blue planet streaked with white clouds.

A comet is a lump of icy rock, usually from the outer solar system.

BLAST OFF!

A rocket blasts off from its launch pad and soars into the sky with flames streaming from its engines. As it climbs higher and higher, the air around it becomes thinner and thinner until there is none at all. The rocket has reached space.

Rocket power

When people wanted to launch machines into space, they had to invent rockets to carry them there. Only rockets are powerful enough to escape the pull of Earth's gravity.

Staging

A rocket is made up of parts called stages. When each stage has used up its fuel, it falls away to save weight. The rest of the rocket goes on into space. The top of the rocket then opens, and a spacecraft comes out. Some spacecraft circle Earth. Others are carried deeper into space by more powerful rockets.

ALL TYPES OF ROCKETS

A-CLASS
Height: 110 feet (33.5m)
Carried the first Russian satellite into space in 1957; the first living creature (a dog named Laika) in the same year; the first human being, Yuri Gagarin, in 1961

REDSTONE
Height: 80 feet (24m)
Carried the first American astronauts into space in 1961

SATURN V
Height: 365 feet (111m)
Carried Apollo spacecraft and astronauts to the Moon between 1969 and 1972

Every spacecraft and satellite sent into space was carried there by a rocket. The first rockets were relatively small and could only lift a small weight. So the first spacecraft and satellites had to be small, too. As people learned more about how to make rockets and how to launch them, the rockets became bigger and more powerful. Bigger rockets can launch bigger spacecraft. The biggest rocket ever built was the American *Saturn V* Moon rocket. (The "V" stands for "5.")

Mission stages

1. The booster rockets quickly burn up their fuel and fall away.

2. The first stage falls away when it has used up its fuel, and engines in the second stage fire to carry the rocket farther into space.

3. The second stage falls away next, then the third stage takes over.

4. Finally, the rocket's nose opens, and the satellite is launched.

5. The satellite's solar panels open in space.

SPACE LAUNCH SYSTEM
Height: 384 feet (117m) Designed to carry humans to Mars in 2030. The first unmanned test launch is planned for 2019.

GOING TO THE MOON

In July 1969, millions of people all over the world turned on their televisions at the same time. They were watching something that had never ever been seen before—an astronaut climbing out of a spacecraft that had just landed on the Moon. It was the first time that anyone from Earth had walked on another world.

When the astronaut Neil Armstrong stepped onto the dusty surface of the Moon, he was farther away from home than any other explorer had ever been.

Shuttle mission

On later Moon missions, astronauts took a special car to the Moon called a Lunar Rover, or Moon Buggy. It helped them get around the Moon's rocky surface more easily.

13

APOLLO SPACECRAFT

The Apollo spacecraft was made up of three parts, called modules. The Lunar Module was the only part of the spacecraft that landed on the Moon. The Command Module was the only part that came back to Earth. The spacecraft had to carry everything that the astronauts needed for their mission—including the air that they breathed.

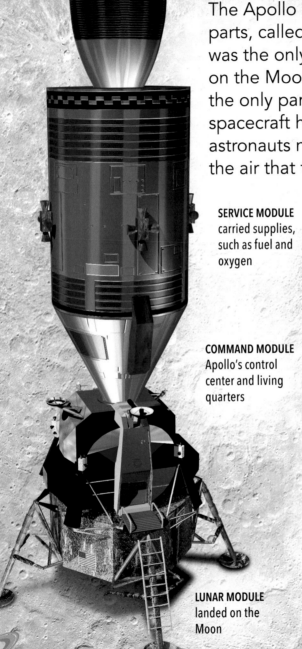

SERVICE MODULE
carried supplies, such as fuel and oxygen

COMMAND MODULE
Apollo's control center and living quarters

LUNAR MODULE
landed on the Moon

The Moon is our closest neighbor in space, but it is still 239,000 miles (384,400km) away. Altogether, 27 astronauts have flown to the Moon, and 12 have landed on its dusty surface.

APOLLO MOON MISSION

1. Flames shot from the five engines at the bottom of the *Saturn V* rocket. Then it slowly rose off the launch pad and climbed into the sky.

5. The astronauts explored the Moon's surface and collected rocks. They also raised the American flag. There is no breeze on the Moon, so the flag was held open by a stiff wire. The flag–and the astronauts' footprints–are still on the Moon.

2. The Command and Service Modules separated from the *Saturn V* rocket. They turned around and joined with the Lunar Module.

6. To leave the Moon, the Lunar Module split in two. Its top half blasted off, using the bottom as a launch pad.

3. The Apollo spacecraft then went on into space. It took three days for the astronauts to travel to the Moon.

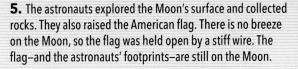

7. The Lunar Module linked with the Command Module. It was then cut loose because it was not needed any more.

4. Two astronauts floated down a tunnel into the Lunar Module and flew it to the Moon. The third stayed in the Command Module.

8. The Command Module separated from the Service Module. It glowed brightly in the sky as it entered the air around Earth. Parachutes opened to slow it down before it splashed into the ocean. The crew was soon picked up by a waiting ship.

SPACE STATIONS

In the future, astronauts will visit the planets. Researchers are now working out how to send people to Mars. But before this can happen, engineers need to learn how to build spacecraft for flights lasting years instead of days or weeks, and scientists need to study how very long space flights affect astronauts.

The International Space Station (ISS)

The ISS is a large spacecraft that has been in orbit around Earth since 1998. Astronauts from all over the world travel to the ISS to work on research or conduct experiments or repairs in space. They can live on the ISS for many months at a time —luckily the ISS has two bathrooms, a gym, plenty of food, and even a phone for the astronauts to call home!

Maybe one day you will be able to visit a space station or take a trip to the Moon!

THE SPACE SHUTTLE

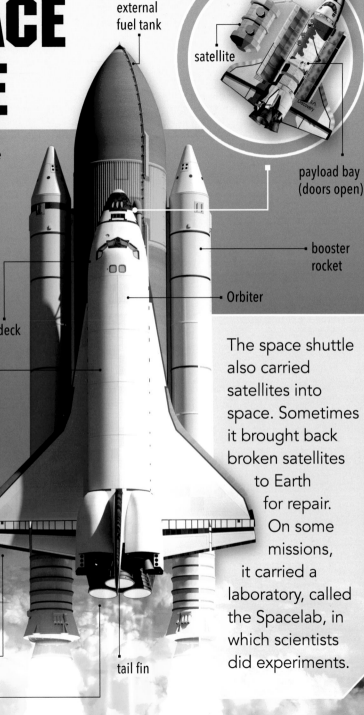

external fuel tank

satellite

payload bay (doors open)

The space shuttle was one of the most complicated machines ever built. It could fly in the air like an aircraft and also in space like a rocket. It was used to take astronauts to and from the International Space Station.

booster rocket

Orbiter

flight deck

payload bay (doors closed)

The space shuttle also carried satellites into space. Sometimes it brought back broken satellites to Earth for repair. On some missions, it carried a laboratory, called the Spacelab, in which scientists did experiments.

The main part of the shuttle was a spacecraft with wings called the Orbiter. It was carried into space by three large rocket engines and two booster rockets.

wings

tail fin

rocket engines

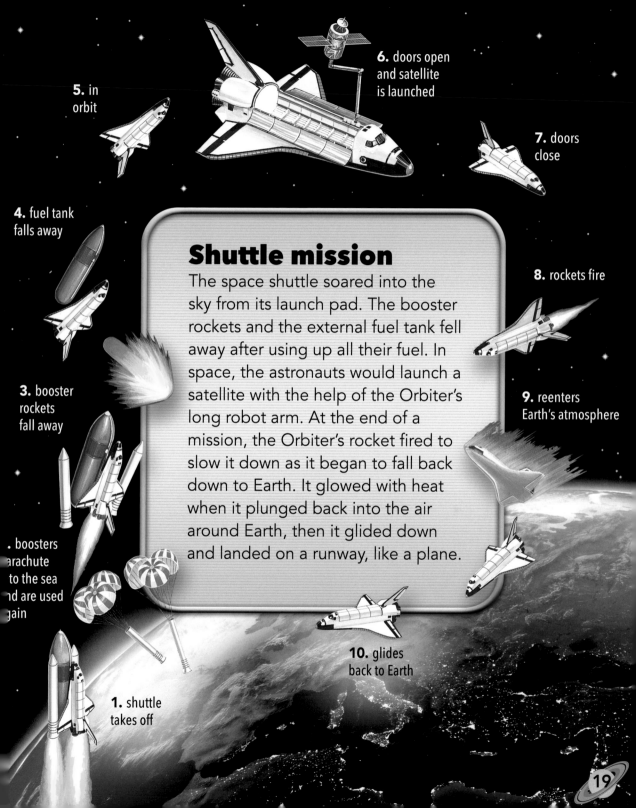

6. doors open and satellite is launched

5. in orbit

7. doors close

4. fuel tank falls away

Shuttle mission

The space shuttle soared into the sky from its launch pad. The booster rockets and the external fuel tank fell away after using up all their fuel. In space, the astronauts would launch a satellite with the help of the Orbiter's long robot arm. At the end of a mission, the Orbiter's rocket fired to slow it down as it began to fall back down to Earth. It glowed with heat when it plunged back into the air around Earth, then it glided down and landed on a runway, like a plane.

8. rockets fire

3. booster rockets fall away

9. reenters Earth's atmosphere

. boosters arachute to the sea nd are used gain

10. glides back to Earth

1. shuttle takes off

SHUTTLE POWER

Most rockets and spacecraft are used only once. This is an incredibly expensive way of sending machines and people into space—no one would build a jumbo jet and throw it away after only one flight! A rocket-powered spacecraft called a space shuttle was different because it could be used over and over again. Unfortunately, the space shuttle wasn't safe enough to continue using. Now, astronauts travel to the ISS in a Russian spacecraft, called a *Soyuz*. This spacecraft cannot be reused; it returns to Earth by falling through the sky with a big parachute to soften the landing.

Space junk

Space junk is a serious problem for astronauts working in space. Parts of old rockets and broken satellites still orbit Earth. If they collide, the fuel inside them may explode, sending pieces of metal flying in all directions.

Astronauts weigh nothing in space. When they leave their spacecraft, they have to clip themselves to it so that they don't float away. This astronaut is repairing a broken satellite. His feet are safely clipped to the space shuttle's long robot arm.

WORKING IN SPACE

Each day's work onboard a space vehicle is set out in the flight plan for the mission. A typical mission may take ten days.

The ISS is in microgravity conditions. That means it almost has no gravity at all. Astronauts and all the objects on the station float—unless they are strapped down!

Shuttle astronauts have around 100 different types of food to choose from. Some food is dried and has to be mixed with water. Drinks are sucked through tubes so drops of liquid don't float around the cabin.

ISS mission

People do different jobs on the space station. The commander is in charge of the station. Flight engineers and mission specialists are trained to do a particular job on a mission, such as launching a satellite.

Sleeping bags are stuck to the cabin walls so that they don't float around. The astronauts wear a mask to block out the light. They are woken by music, beamed up from Earth.

The commander, pilot, and mission specialists are all astronauts. Extra crew members, called payload specialists, are not. They may be scientists or doctors who do experiments in the Spacelab, or engineers who operate special equipment.

Astronauts have to clip themselves to the seat when they use the toilet, or they might float away.

SPACE SUITS

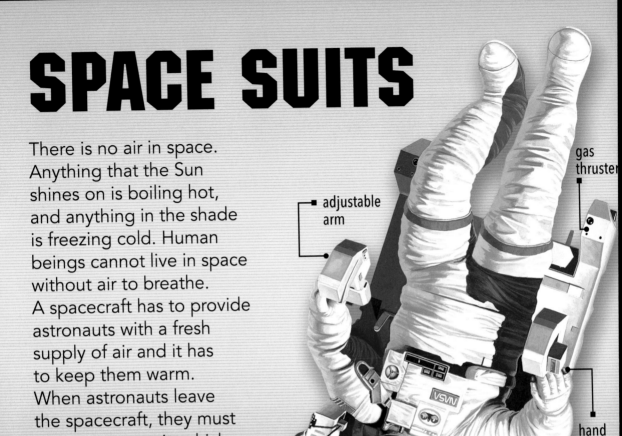

There is no air in space. Anything that the Sun shines on is boiling hot, and anything in the shade is freezing cold. Human beings cannot live in space without air to breathe. A spacecraft has to provide astronauts with a fresh supply of air and it has to keep them warm. When astronauts leave the spacecraft, they must wear a space suit, which performs the same task.

adjustable arm

gas thruster

hand controller

nitrogen gas tank

gas thruster

Manned Maneuvring Unit (MMU) helps astronauts fly around outside the shuttle.

Putting on a space suit

This space suit is called the space shuttle EMU, which is short for Extravehicular Mobility Unit. The suit has a special backpack that keeps fresh air flowing through the suit.

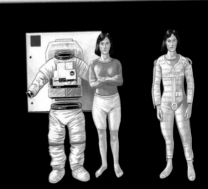

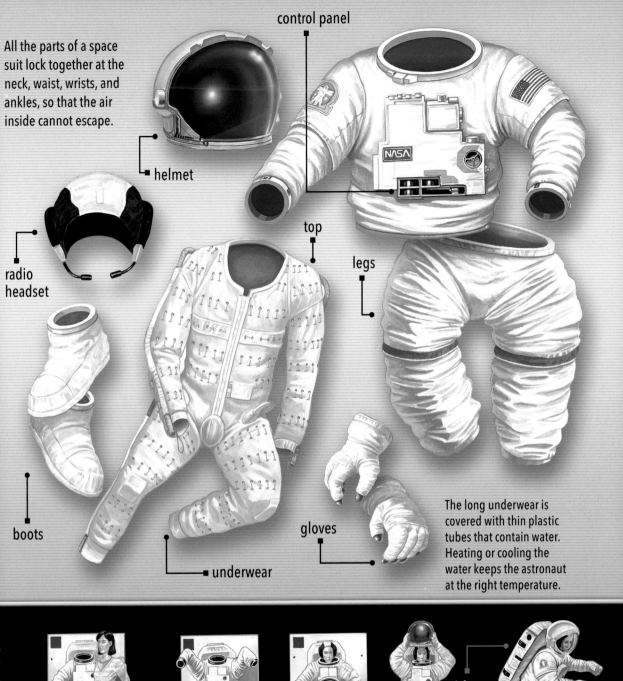

control panel

All the parts of a space suit lock together at the neck, waist, wrists, and ankles, so that the air inside cannot escape.

helmet

radio headset

top

legs

boots

underwear

gloves

The long underwear is covered with thin plastic tubes that contain water. Heating or cooling the water keeps the astronaut at the right temperature.

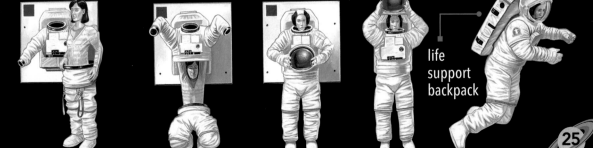

life support backpack

EYES IN SPACE

Weather satellites watch Earth and its weather all day and night. Other satellites beam telephone calls and television programs all over the world. There are hundreds of satellites orbiting Earth. They have become so important, it's difficult to imagine our world without them.

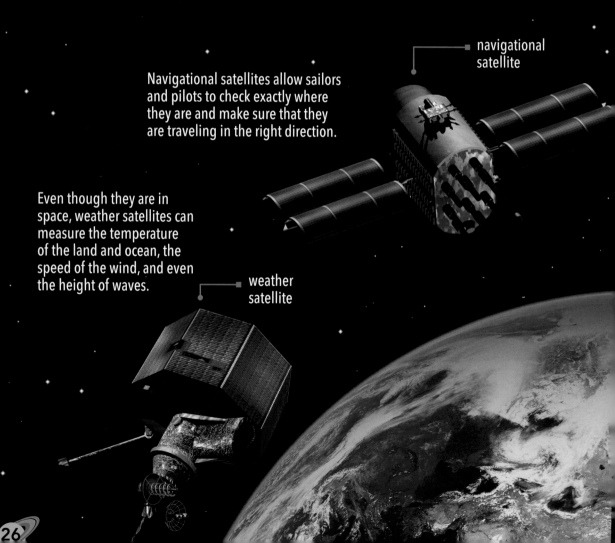

navigational satellite

Navigational satellites allow sailors and pilots to check exactly where they are and make sure that they are traveling in the right direction.

Even though they are in space, weather satellites can measure the temperature of the land and ocean, the speed of the wind, and even the height of waves.

weather satellite

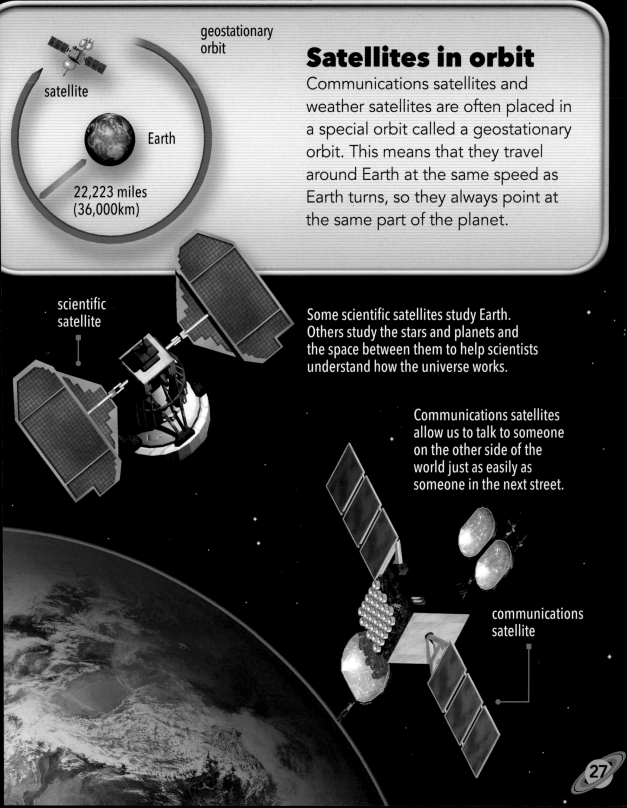

geostationary orbit

satellite

Earth

22,223 miles
(36,000km)

Satellites in orbit

Communications satellites and weather satellites are often placed in a special orbit called a geostationary orbit. This means that they travel around Earth at the same speed as Earth turns, so they always point at the same part of the planet.

scientific satellite

Some scientific satellites study Earth. Others study the stars and planets and the space between them to help scientists understand how the universe works.

Communications satellites allow us to talk to someone on the other side of the world just as easily as someone in the next street.

communications satellite

THE HUBBLE TELESCOPE

Stars look so beautiful because they twinkle like diamonds, but twinkling makes it difficult for astronomers to see them clearly through a telescope. Twinkling is caused by swirling streams of warm and cold air around Earth bending the starlight in different ways. A telescope in space has the best view of the stars because there is no air in space to make them twinkle. The biggest telescope in space is the Hubble Telescope which was launched from a space shuttle in 1990.

Repairing the Hubble

Before repair

After repair

When the Hubble was launched, astronomers discovered that its view was blurred because it had a faulty mirror. Shuttle astronomers mended the telescope in 1993. Since then, the Hubble has been sending clear pictures back to Earth.

The Hubble has two large, flat solar panels—one on each side. They make electricity from sunlight in order to power the Hubble's instruments. It sends its pictures to Earth by radio.

SPACE PROBES

Every 175 years, the giant planets Jupiter, Saturn, Uranus, and Neptune line up. This means that a spacecraft can visit all of them in one trip. Two space probes, *Voyagers 1* and *2*, traveled all the way to these planets. They sent back some of the most beautiful pictures we have ever seen—of stormy orange and white clouds over Jupiter, volcanoes erupting on Jupiter's moons, and the broad, flat rings around Saturn.

Journey to the Stars

Tiny space probes have visited all eight planets in the solar system. A few have even left the solar system altogether. *Pioneer 10*, launched in 1972, is the farthest away. The last, very weak signal was received from it in 2003, when it was more than six billion miles (9.6 billion km) from Earth. A final attempt to contact the probe in 2006 received no response.

MARINER
Mariner 9 orbited Mars in 1971, and *Mariner 10* visited Venus and Mercury in 1974.

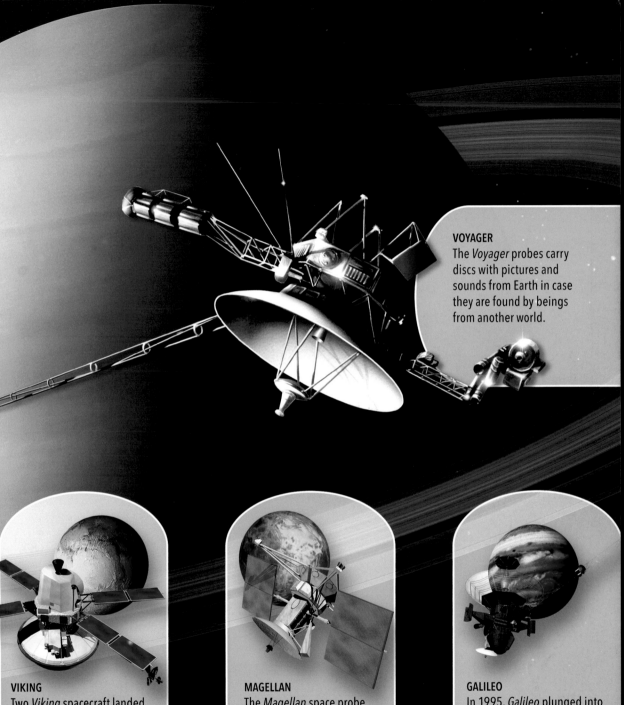

VOYAGER
The *Voyager* probes carry discs with pictures and sounds from Earth in case they are found by beings from another world.

VIKING
Two *Viking* spacecraft landed on Mars in 1976 and tested the soil for signs of life.

MAGELLAN
The *Magellan* space probe visited Venus in 1989. Its instruments made a map of Venus's surface.

GALILEO
In 1995, *Galileo* plunged into the gases around Jupiter, sending information back to Earth. In 2003, *Galileo*'s mission ended.

GLOSSARY

astronaut A space traveler.

atmosphere The layer of gases that surround a planet or moon. Earth's atmosphere, or air, is made mainly of three gases—nitrogen, oxygen, and carbon dioxide.

booster An extra rocket used to help launch a larger rocket or the space shuttle.

capsule A small spacecraft with just enough room inside to fit in the crew.

countdown The preparations for the launch of a rocket as a clock ticks backward to zero—the moment when the rocket fires and takes off.

EVA Extra Vehicular Activity—another name for a spacewalk.

gravity The force that pulls everything down to the ground and keeps the planets in orbit around the Sun and satellites in orbit around planets.

launch pad The platform that a rocket or space shuttle stands on for takeoff.

moon A small world that orbits a planet. A moon is a natural satellite.

Moon Buggy An electric car used by some of the Apollo astronauts to drive around on the Moon.

NASA National Aeronautics and Space Administration—the organization that runs American space flights.

orbit The path of a satellite around a planet or a planet around the Sun.

payload Cargo carried by a rocket or space shuttle.

planet A world in orbit around the Sun.

reentry Coming back into, or reentering, Earth's atmosphere from space.

satellite An object in orbit around a planet. A moon is a natural satellite. A spacecraft is an artificial satellite.

solar system The Sun and everything that orbits it, including the planets, their moons, asteroids, and comets.

space probe An unmanned spacecraft sent far away from Earth to find out more about the Sun, the planets, or their moons.

spaceship Any spacecraft that carries people.

space station A large, manned spacecraft that is kept in space for several years.

space suit The special clothing worn by astronauts to protect them when they go outside their spacecraft.

splashdown Landing a spacecraft in the ocean.

thruster A tiny rocket engine that fires to nudge a spacecraft into a new position.

INDEX

A
A-Class rocket 10
Apollo mission 14–15
Apollo spacecraft 10, 14–15
Armstrong, Neil 12
asteroid 7
astronaut 10, 13, 14, 15, 16, 18, 19, 21, 22–23, 24

B
booster rocket 10, 11, 18, 19

CD
comet 6, 7
Command Module 14, 15

EF
Extravehicular Mobility Unit (EMU) 24, 25
flight plan 22
fuel tank 18, 19

G
Gagarin, Yuri 10
galaxy 6, 7
Galileo probe 31
geostationary orbit 27
gravity 6, 8, 22

HIJ
Hubble Space Telescope 28–29
Jupiter 6, 30, 31

L
Laika 10
launch pad 8, 14, 15, 32

life-support backpack 25
Lunar Module 14, 15

M
Magellan probe 31
Manned Maneuvering Unit (MMU) 24, 25
Mariner probe 30
Mars 6, 10, 16, 30
Mercury 6, 31
Milky Way 5
Moon 10, 12, 14, 15, 17
Moon Buggy 12

N
Neptune 7, 30

O
orbit 6, 7, 16, 19, 20, 26, 27
orbiter 18, 19

PQ
payload 18, 23
Pioneer probe 30
planet 4, 6–7
probe 30–31

R
Redstone rocket 10
reentry 19
robot arm 19, 21
rocket 8, 9, 10, 11, 15, 18, 19, 20

S
satellite 10, 11, 18, 19, 21, 23, 26–27
Saturn 7, 30
Saturn V rocket 10, 14
Service Module 14, 15
solar system 6, 7, 30
space junk 20
Spacelab 18, 23

Space launch system rocket 10
space probe 30–31
space shuttle 18, 19, 20, 21, 24, 28
space station 16–17, 22–23
space suit 24–25
stages (of a rocket) 11
star 4, 6, 27, 28
Sun 6

T
thruster 24
toilet 23

U
Uranus 7, 30

VWXYZ
Venus 6, 30, 31
Viking probe 30
Voyager probe 30, 31